Illuminated Soul:

A Collection of Poetic Reflections

Nikí R. Ferguson

Blu Fountain Streams Publications

Illuminated Soul: A Collection of Poetic Reflections
© 2021 Nikí R. Ferguson

The Holy Bible. New King James Version. Thomas Nelson, Inc. 1990. American Bible Society

Published by Blu Fountain Streams Publications
Flint, Michigan 48507

Cover design by Nikí R. Ferguson

ISBN: 978-0-578-34299-3

Printed in the United States
For Worldwide Publication

Acknowledgements

To my husband: thank you for your love and patience throughout my creative process.

To my family, friends, and colleagues: thank you for your continued support along the way. Your conversation and inspiration have been an important part of my process.

To my mentors and accountability partners: thank you for your willingness to listen and advise, boosting me beyond excuses and into a positive creative mindset.

To my AWAOA community: thank you for your encouragement, insight, and motivation. You have contributed to my development and progression.

I thank God for His grace and giving me wings to fly.

Your voice is like a fingerprint.

It is a part of everything you touch.

When people hear you, they know your voice.

-- Nikí Ferguson

Table of Contents

Enlighten

Lord, I Thank You

Lord, I thank You that I have breath in my body.

Lord, I thank You that it is You that's in control.

Lord, I thank You that You are the great creator.

Lord, I thank You that it's You I must behold.

Shining Light

Continue to work on me.

In me,

through me,

with me.

Show me Your light as I continue to walk

through this tunnel of life.

Allowing my light to shine bright.

Restore Me

Restore me

to my most creative self.

Restore me

from the noise outside myself.

Restore me

from the noise inside myself.

Restore me

to my best physical self.

Restore me

to my mentally strengthened self.

Restore me

to be my truest to myself.

Restore me

to my greatest potential.

Sometimes, you must find the right power source to
get your desired results.
-- Nikí Ferguson

Sunbeam

As the daylight sun beams upon us,

My eyes are open to the beauty that is you.

As the vibrant colors make their appearance,

There is no pretense.

You are all natural.

There is nothing false about you.

Breathtaking Sunrise

This morning,
the sunrise
peaking over the bed of clouds
was breathtaking.

Blinded

I was blinded by the glory of the sun this morning.

It reminded me of how bright the *Son* should shine in my life.

Rising Glow

This morning's sky subdued your light.

But even through its haze it didn't diminish your rising glow.

Your grace still shined through like an iridescent globe.

Natural Refreshing

There is something about the sound the water makes when the waves move across the shore. The continuous shushing brings the calming effect you could fall asleep to.

It puts you in the mode of a quiet, peaceful place. One where you could tune everything out and put you at ease for the time being, while washing away the cares of this world.

The water's fluid movement constantly flows even in its subtle wavy stillness moving only slightly to the eye. You still sway in motion with the water itself.

Imagine being able to float on the surface like a boat. The lightness of your body being carried away with the streams of motion. Feeling the water drift over your frame restoring healing properties to your skin and muscles.

Experiencing the weightlessness and the heaviness of the water simultaneously. Knowing, while floating, the water could pull you down at any given moment from its current. Yet the nourishment of the water supports and embodies your spiritual nature bringing about a natural refreshing.

Mornings Melody

I awoke one morning

to hear the birds singing

their melodic songs of beauty.

Conversing with each other

from across the meadows,

echoing their unique sounds.

Perched in their trees

to a day where spring

seemed so far away.

With an overcast view of the sun

extends the briskness of morning,

Still, they sang with an exuberance of life.

Basking in the flourishing flowers of spring

where they drank from the dew

of honeysuckled petals.

Finally, springing up

soaring above the horizon,

doing what they were created for.

Fluidly flying with the graceful glide

of the wind beneath their wings.

Refreshing

I love the sound the water makes

when the waves crash against the shore.

The feeling it brings is peaceful and soothing.

It glistens from the sun gleaming overhead.

The lights reflection dancing, fluidly moving,

rippling with brilliance.

A refreshing breeze captured from the wind

overshadows the warmth on a heated day.

While the rustling leaves mimic

the fluttering chatter of a steady rain.

Seagulls fly elegantly through the air

soaring with the wind beneath their wings.

A gentle gust tussling my hair

sweeping draft brushing my face.

Looking up, I bask in the glow.

The sun beaming down,

The wind whisking my skirt to and fro.

The sand encasing my settling feet.

Receiving the properties of the earth.

Externally, I am receiving my healing.

Internally, my spirit is lifting.

Moonstruck

The moon this night hovered over,

making me feel as if I were one with it.

The silver lighting glowed as it illuminated the glistening waters,

rippling just slightly.

The coolness of the night drifted over me,

bring a sense of comfort.

There was a feeling of peace and calm

as I reflected over this vision.

Allowing me to disconnect from the cares of the day.

October

Welcome October.

Where the briskness of the cool air dances with Indian summers,

mixed with exuberant colors of fall.

Where the sunlight highlights hues of burgundy dreams,

sun kissed amber and tangerine

cascades with embraced warmth.

Falling leaves mimic the sound of rain

as the trees shed in the breeze.

The flavorful aromas of pumpkin spice and apple cider prance in the air.

Fall is my favorite time of year.

It's the shedding of old skins for new beginnings.

Welcome October.

Your Embrace

With arms stretched wide,

I feel You embracing me.

The songs I sing

flow through me

to exalt You.

The urge to dance

with arms uplifted

as the music carries me.

I feel the swaying

as if I were levitating,

encapsulated by the melodies.

My spirit is elevating

by the lengthening of my arms,

to the tips of my fingers.

Seemingly rising through the air

as if gliding gracefully,

like the extension of the eagle's wings.

You are moving through my being

capturing the puppet in me as if

structuring my movements for Your praise.

I imagine if I could fly.

I would fly through the air spinning

pirouettes until my arms were

outstretched in surrender

at Your presence.

Comforted by Your grace,

draped in Your covering.

Experiencing Your weightlessness,

only to be surrounded and evaporate,

captured by Your embrace.

Grateful

Grateful

for another day to live.

That the electrical synapses

in my brain fire

each morning I awake,

brand new to open

closed eyes.

To see past the fog

from my dreaming state.

To process information

without hesitation,

without confusion.

Grateful

to inhale

through clear lungs.

To breathe fresh air

without inhibition.

To exhale

without restriction.

Grateful

to recognize the autonomic operation

of the respiratory function.

Something casually

taken for granted.

Grateful

for a beating heart

that blood flows freely.

Pumping through

the arterial walls of life.

Grateful

for additional moments

to see the light of day.

To experience the changing seasons,

as each day's trajectory transforms

the newness of another day's grace.

Another day's purpose.

Another day of life.

Dare to dream beyond the stars and into eternity.
-- Niki Ferguson

Masterpiece

It starts with a word,
A line
And then a verse.

It starts with a sound,
A look
A voice
An image.

It starts with a moment,
A feeling
A memory
A dream.

It starts with a person,
A place
An event
A movement.

In the end,
It becomes
A masterpiece.

Poetry

Poetry is like fresh air as it briskly brushes my face.

Poetry is like the cool water washing over my skin as a refreshed anointing.

Poetry is like the sight and sound of autumns colorful leaves falling, whispering before reaching the ground.

Poetry is like the vibration of a heart felt laugh that's good for the soul.

Poetry is like the tingling sensation your skin feels from a lover's touch.

Poetry is like the butterflies in your stomach from that precious first kiss.

Poetry is like the fluidity of movement swaying from a dance.

Poetry is like the symbols sweet ping, the saxophones smooth velvet grove.

Poetry is like the symphony; each line plays emotional melodies as thoughts fluctuate in harmony.

Poetry is like the waves of the sea.

Sometimes chaotic and sometimes at peace.

Poetry is like a roller coaster ride that carries you through loops of emotions.

Poetry is like a long-ago childhood friend.

You remember them with fond memories and when reconnected, you didn't skip a beat.

Poetry found me when I wasn't looking.

It acquainted itself with me in a way I didn't know I was missing.

Extraordinary

I used to think I was ordinary.

Sitting in a place of constant introspection.

Then my mind shifted.

I woke up from a place of self-reflection.

There is nothing ordinary about me.

I am extraordinary.

I only had to believe.

She

She walked into the room.

Quietly, she stood in the doorway.

Studied the room to measure the temperature.

She moved carefully, not to immediately attract attention.

She walked, shoulders square, chin lifted, eyes alert.

She was wearing a semi-fitted shimmering mocha dress with a boat-cut neckline and ¾ length sleeves.

A calf length A-line skirt with a split up the mid-thigh that swayed when she moved.

Even though her aura glowed, she was mysterious.

The room was occupied with many whose air was high, chatting amongst themselves.

Everyone dressed in their best After 5 evening attire.

Those in the room seemingly having an elevated position.

The ambiance of the room was lit well above the low brilliance of the chandeliers.

Seated in the corner, her eyes calibrating her next destination.

Yet she watched.

Waiting.

Like a wallflower waiting to be plucked.

The butterflies in her stomach began to flutter

The anticipation rising as she anxiously counted down the seconds ticking in her heart.

Finally,

The spotlight panned on the speaker of the room

A hush fell over the crowd.

The introduction came.

She stood and slightly brushed her dress to smooth it.

The spotlight followed as she was led to the crystal podium.

All eyes on her.

She lowered her head briefly as if to say a quick prayer.

When she raised it, her eyes scanned to room.

This moment was hers.

She smiled.

She opened her mouth to speak.

Who was she?

When I opened my eyes from the slumber of this dream, I realized...

She was me.

The words whispered to her.

She spoke them in a poem.

The poem became music.

The music became movement.

She became the movement of the poem.

--Nikí Ferguson

Desire

Selfish

In my selfishness,

I have discovered

I prefer not to share you with anyone.

Yesterday's Emotion

Yesterday I faltered.

I was overcome.

Tears streaming,

salted with discouragement.

Repeatedly gasping for air.

Losing my breath

from trying to hold it together.

Trying to keep my heart from exploding.

Trying to keep my tongue from lashing out.

Hurt by your blindness,

praying you would get it.

Overcome with emotion

from fear of losing you.

Disconnected

She reached for him.

Searching his eyes,

her fingers gently touched his face.

The other hand lay on his chest,

feeling the rhythm of his heartbeat.

Feeling his distance,

she thought to kiss him.

Afraid of his rejection,

she tried anyway.

Even his kisses felt distant.

Disconnected.

When a Man Loves a Woman

When a man loves a woman,

he looks through the windows of her eyes.

He's committed to knowing her intimate mind.

He holds her in high esteem.

His care for her is most precious.

He is her truest friend.

He's connected to her soul.

His thoughts merge with hers.

When a man truly loves a woman

he is the guardian and defender of her heart

and keeps her close to his.

He comforts her during sorrow.

He is the strength behind her weakness.

He bares her burdens.

He loves her beyond her faults.

When a man completely loves a woman,

he perceives her manifested desires.

He sacrifices to meet her needs.

He puts hers before his own.

He is the protector of their home,

the seeker of her safety.

He is the cultivator of her dreams.

When a man sincerely loves a woman,

he finds ways to lift her spirits.

Pampers her affections.

He is not neglectful or seedy.

His exploration of her is continuous.

He romanticizes her essence.

His praises of her are worthy of her elevation.

His emphasis is in her happiness.

When a man triumphantly loves a woman,

He endeavors to build his Queen a palace.

He reaches ahead to solidify their future.

His arms strive to carry her into eternity.

When a man loves a woman.

Kiss Me

Kiss me.

Brush against my lips like a whisper.

Soft, slow, and tender.

Taste my lips as if drinking from the honey suckles nectar.

Kiss me.

Until my heart grows full of your ravenous appetite.

Until we are breathing as one vessel

Until our bodies heat meld us together.

Kiss me.

Until I swoon from weakened knees.

Until the tingling sensation stirs my core.

Until it feels as though the earth is melting beneath my feet.

Until that moments vision is painted with the constellation of stars.

Kiss me.

As if time and space stopped momentarily for our embrace.

As if you were my sun and I, your moon burning with anticipation of the next eclipse.

Kiss me.

As if your kiss were the oxygen necessary for my survival.

As if it were the last impression of you, I would remember for eternity.

Kiss me.

Touch me with your eyes.

Draw me in with your secrets.

Breathe into my soul.

Love's Expectancy

My body yields for your extended embrace.

Your touch leaves behind remnants of your presence.

The impression left by your kisses causes my lips to crave more.

My heart quickens with expectation of your love.

You call me beautiful,

even when I don't feel it.

Vulnerability of Fear

There is a time when you are most vulnerable.

You want to be vulnerable in front of your mate,

but you have a difficult time expressing those feelings.

You take your vulnerability and hide it thinking you are protecting yourself.

Shielding yourself from something that is bigger than you.

Fear plays a big part in communication.

Fear of rejection, fear of misunderstanding.

Fear of the unknown.

But how do you get someone to see you

if you continue to hide behind the invisible mask that is you?

Illuminated Passion

Take me to a place where you occupy my space.

Your nature engulfs me, filling the loins of my purpose.

Take me to a higher plain, my body flying to greater heights.

Your touch leaves my body smoldering.

Magnetically aligned in our kinetic energy.

Struck by the spark of your kindling.

Waiting for the open flame, ignite me with your passion.

Our sizzling remnants leaving lasting impressions scorched in loves surface.

Our intertwined auras locked, inhabit our destiny,

where the cascading stars gift us with our own constellation.

And moons light illuminates our passion.

Soul Searching

As you look into my eyes,

are you peering into the depths of my soul

or are you only seeing the surface?

Soul Speak

I melted back into his arms.

My head nestled under his chin.

He embraced me from behind.

My arms wrapped into his.

Enticing me with his words.

Whispering sweet nothings in my ear.

His voice sends shivers down my spine.

The sound of his vibrato penetrating my heart.

He spoke life into my soul.

Soul Step

Their hips sway together with the slow tempo.

Fingers snapping at the beat of the music.

Bodies close, stepping in unison.

His arms resting on her hips.

Hers, resting around his neck.

This moment made them want to get closer.

Unaware of their surroundings,

the strobing lights glittered in the atmosphere.

Only the music fills their ears.

The way he smells melts her insides.

Like the petals of a rose; her skin, soft and supple to the touch.

The way she feels pressed against him makes his flesh weak.

Her head nestles into the nook of his neck.

His sway dips with the beat of the slow grind, tells her his story.

Sensual friction building through the swiveling of their hips.

The dip of his grind deepening at the knees.

Her body conforming to his soul step.

His lips nuzzle against her ear.

His arms form a cocoon around her back.

Her aura encased by his essence.

She absorbs the rhythmic sensation from his breathing.

Her insides dripping with desire.

Their bodies moving as one vessel.

Passion overflowing on the dance floor.

Imagine a Man

Can you imagine a man?

A man searching for his mate.

Searching for his equal.

A man, not easily tamed.

When he meets the woman,

he searches her.

Her character, her warmth.

Her strength, her heart.

Imagine a man falling.

Quickly nestling into home.

Connecting to his partner.

Intimately transforming together.

Imagine a man

whose soul becomes linked.

Whose found the missing lock to his key.

A man who finds his perfect fit.

The one to which he chooses to cling.

Imagine when he encloses her hand.

Looks into her eyes,

tunes others out and says,

"it's you I must protect."

His choice becomes evident.

Imagine the man.

Not just himself

but his family to preserve.

The one he searched for.

The one he prayed for.

His Queen and his lair.

His sanctuary.

Imagine a man.

Now the protector

looking over the world

with clearer vision

laying a plan,

the one he envisioned.

Imagine this man.

His sacrifice to build

as he molds his life.

Leaving all else behind

motivated beyond mankind.

Now,

imagine a man

on constant alert

because he has more to fight for.

Counting the cost priceless,

more value to lose if he doesn't.

Imagine a man

looking behind him

from scrutiny's eyes.

The world full of ridicule,

constantly revealing his mistakes.

Condemning the choices he makes.

Image a man

not above judgement

but always being judged

by his ordered steps.

Steps only he can face.

Imagine this man

facing his giants.

Destroying the daggers

intended to slay him,

armed with his sword

guarding his post,

taking a stand.

Imagine a man.

Fight

Would you fight for me?

Fight for our love.

All that we've built.

Would you throw it all away

over some bullshit?

Would you choose to run?

Hide behind pride,

instead of using that energy

to face the demons inside.

Seeking to make amends,

releasing our past offense.

Would you fight?

Would you fight for us?

Take seriously the vows we took.

For better, for worse.

In sickness and health.

Forsaking all others.

Cover us from that which is imperfect.

Protect us from the world outside.

Whose only impulse is to judge and scrutinize.

Whose only desire is to tear us apart.

Whose only agenda is to thrive in our demise.

Would you fight?

For richer, for poorer.

Through hills and valleys.

Through bouts of anxiety and fear.

To keep promises made.

To build from the ground up.

Striving to build better.

To open the door to our future.

Would you fight?

Fight to remove the very mountain that stands.

Stands in the way of our happiness.

Would you look at me the way you first fell?

Pursue me now the way our love story tells?

Would you fight?

To allow our love to grow.

Yet stand still in the earth,

roots standing firmly planted,

so that nothing can sway us from our futures
destiny...

and those who try, will recognize our fight.

Humbling

Be the most genuine person you can be to inspire those who are watching you.
-- Niki Ferguson

Ode to our Parents

Little children see their parents as superhuman.

They build them up because they have to look high to see them.

We may marvel at all the things they do, but we also scowl at the things they don't do.

As we get older, we start to see they are not perfect.

They have flaws.

They make mistakes.

But what we have are examples.

Examples of going to work every day (we hope anyway).

Examples of taking care of their families.

We see the example of their sacrifices to make sure we have what we need.

Many times, we don't see what goes behind the getting up and going to work.

And as children, we don't understand all the trials and tribulations of life.

We don't always see what it takes to set an example.

Our parents are there to give us guidance and guidelines.

To make the hard choices for us.

As children, it's easy to go against the grain because we don't see what they see and haven't been where they've been.

It's easy to say, "you don't understand how I feel!" or "you don't get it!"

Until it's time for us to step into their shoes.

There are boundaries and lessons our parents are commanded to teach us.

Whether we know it or not, the road to adulthood isn't easy.

As they go through life, they too, are trying to figure it out.

At some point in our lives, we do realize our parents are human.

They have feelings and human problems.

They have human choices and may not always get it right.

As adults, we see the reality setting in.

The transitional change as child to caregiver.

We now experience the challenges.

We now make the decisions.

We now make the necessary sacrifices.

As a young person, I didn't always understand why you had to save money instead of spending it.

I didn't understand the bigger picture.

But I watched as my parents went to work.

I watched the work ethic.

I took note of the no nonsense mentality.

Walking into adulthood meant change, sacrifice and responsibility.

Making hard, but necessary decisions.

Being the bad guy.

In that way, we know you are proud of us and the people we have become.

Whether they are great or small accomplishments.

We know as our parent you may worry about us and our decisions, but you allow us to make them.

Like you followed your road, you empower us to follow ours... yes, with some input along the way.

For that we are strong even when we feel weak.

We've had a compass for guidance.

For that we honor you.

*There are times I feel as though I am caught between
my feelings and reality.*

Blue and Black Abstract

I closed my eyes to go to sleep.

My dreams are vivid in color.

As I lay, my mind drifting,

The background is lit in muted amber.

I see dark blue and black in swirling lines.

Usually, I see in colors and pictures.

This time, color, and robust lines.

Robust lines mingling side by side.

Entangled in constant movement.

As the entanglement continues,

My focus fixated to make it out.

The connection between blue and black.

The configuration of wild formations.

The struggles the black lines have with the blue.

Back and forth, the fight in perpetual turmoil.

Rolling circular movements,

resting in continuous broken seconds.

Unbalanced, swaying and contorted,

like figures dancing trying to find their footing.

But, neither is winning.

Now, my sleep interrupted,

only to see the glimpse of a lasted impression.

This picturesque motion visually posed,

as if splattered in an abstract painting.

Colors of Life

It's hard to imagine what another person sees from behind their eyes.

What a person feels in their body as it begins to falter.

You wonder if they feel the light beginning to slowly fade...

If all they can focus on is the complexity of their decline.

Reminded of their former self.

Seeing the shadow of what once was,

now transcending beyond loved ones.

Knowing or unknowing that final fate.

You wonder if the movie reels have been replayed.

If those days are plagued by unfinished stories

or fondly looked back upon as the beauty that was.

You wonder how vivid those colors are seen from within.

If a fixated gaze absorbs the colors of life as it begins to dim.

If it's fear that grips them or peace that embraces them.

You start to think about the fragility of mortality.

Beautiful in its wholeness but like shattered glass,

it cuts deep, picking up the pieces from its splintered
reality.

Immortality does not live in our physical bodies,

but immortality lives on in continuing generations.

God promised everlasting life through Him.

The impression of what it's like when eyes are
closed, never to open again.

What it's like to contemplate life before death.

Whether resting in the eternal sleep of nothingness

or perhaps drawn to an eternal light.

I ponder over the colors of life I see,

appreciating that which surrounds me.

Through decades of relationships built,

I wonder what impression I've left.

How others will remember me...

When I leave this earth,

how the Lord will receive me.

If I've done all He's asked of me.

If I have loved intentionally,

if I have forgiven purposefully,

if I have lived peaceably,

if wisdom followed me,

if creativity embodied me.

If my light has lit the path before me.

Thoughtful, each night I lay down my head,

I still say this silent prayer...

Now I lay me down to sleep

I pray the Lord my soul to keep

If I should die before I wake

I pray the Lord my soul to take.

Human

I am human.

I am perfectly flawed.

Daily, I make mistakes.

Daily, I learn new lessons about myself.

I am a work in progress,

but always progressing.

I am ever evolving from my many layers of
imperfections.

If you cut me, I will bleed.

If you speak disparaging things about me, my spirit
may cringe.

When fiery darts are thrown my way, my flesh will
singe.

You have stigmatized me with your cunning words,

condemned me for past mistakes.

Frozen them in time.

As if to say I am undeserving of forgiveness.

As if to say I am undeserving of newness.

As if to say I am undeserving of happiness.

Your desire is for me to hang my head down in
shame.

I will hold it high and look you straight in the eye.

I will not look away.

I will not bow to your game.

My armor is fit for a King.

And though you might try to pierce it,

no weapon formed against me shall prosper.

In my search for healing,

in my search for wellbeing,

in my search for greatness...

I wake up every morning with the best intentions

to establish gratitude in an ungrateful world.

I look for ways I will matter and make a difference.

Even though you look for ways to shatter them with
your daggers,

my dreams are bigger than your limitations.

Though you may try to measure them with my past
indiscretions,

I am hopeful that my ideas and visions will start
worthwhile conversations.

I am living a life worthy of my own expectations.

I am looking for my best self.

To see that humanity has a soul in the process.

The choices I make don't include the skeptics.

The choices I make are about what makes me
significant,

and how others may be inspired by my established work.

The choices I make are not meant to offer an apology to those who are disapproving.

Who try to involve me in their mockery.

I am building something more precious than your criticism.

More precious than your malice.

Humanity isn't blemish free.

But the world is full of condemnation.

It's filled with obstinate characters using open platforms to inject venom into society.

To downgrade those who pursue greatness.

But greatness does not seek nor need approval.

It simply is.

Greatness breaks the mold.

It isn't counterfeit.

Greatness,

in its enormity,

maximizes strength while recognizing weakness.

While I strive for greatness

and pursue excellence;

I am still Human.

*It's important to know when to be silent and listen
and to speak and be heard.*
-- Nikí Ferguson

More than Enough

As women, we are equipped to carry.

Carry children, households, careers and for some, ministry.

We carry our emotions, our burdens, people's perception of who we are or what we are.

We carry their expectations of us and perceived expectations of ourselves.

We compare ourselves to others not realizing our own value or worth.

It can be draining and overwhelming at times.

Our desire to please others puts limitations on our individual growth.

We begin to please everyone but ourselves, producing a combustible pressure.

I submit, we are more than enough.

We have burdened ourselves far too long.

Cast our cares upon the Lord.

Like a pebble cast into the sea, that may sink into the abyss never to return.

We are equal to.

Not less than.

We are above.

Not beneath.

We stand worthy of honor.

We must walk in it.

Yes, it is easier said than done.

But in our weakness, He strengthens us.

Trust in the Lord with your heart and lean not unto your own understanding. In all your ways acknowledge Him and He shall direct your paths.

Proverbs 3:5-6

Trust that we are more than enough.

For those who have us downtrodden, remember, they are no better or worse than us.

Only the wise counsel will stand in our corner.

When overwhelmed by our burdens, cast our cares. He will carry them and sustain us.

No one can stand in our shoes until they have walked where we have walked.

We answer to only God and our own family.

We are human, as are they.

Not superhuman as we sometimes try.

Hills and valleys will come.

Our trials are our tests.

Our lives are a journey of mistakes, lessons and triumphs.

Though we are not perfect, we can only do our best.

By doing our best, we've already done what He's asked.

We keep going.

Phase out the noise we struggle with.

Don't give people power over you that allows your countenance to change.

Be the We, we are meant to be!

That's the only person we can be.

Undergirded by the God who strengthens us.

Sometimes people judge or make comments because they don't know any better.

And those that know better, don't care.

As we know, people are drastically flawed.

Even those we have higher expectations of.

We are more than others perception of us.

Our power is in our walk.

Our confidence is in holding our head high.

There is boldness in our journey.

I admonish us to remember...

We are more than enough.

Imperfect

I am human

but also imperfect.

I see with imperfect eyes

but pray for perfect vision.

I walk with imperfect legs

but pray for a healthy stride.

I talk with imperfect words

but ask for wisdom before I speak.

I think with an imperfect mind

but ask for understanding.

I hear with imperfect ears

but ask for listening discernment.

I stand with an imperfect frame

but ask for strength to carry heavy burdens.

I feel with an imperfect heart

but ask to love intentionally.

I hurt with imperfect emotions

but ask to forgive daily.

There are times I feel as many do,

but choose not to follow the multitude.

I lean not on my own understanding,

but trust He will carry me through.

Because I am imperfect,

I do not always see that which is before me.

Because I am imperfect,

I must trust that He perfects me as I go.

Because I am imperfect,

I must have the faith of a mustard seed.

Because I am imperfect.

I must walk in humility.

I don't mind that I'm imperfect

because in my imperfect uniqueness,

I look to the One who created me.

Because,

I am perfectly me.

Faith Over Fear

We are healing from a community of suffering.

Humanity has been disturbed by a silent intruder, violently invading fleshly tissues.

Our internal membranes distressed and asphyxiated.

Mortality subjected to an unknown fate, leaving an ocean of bodies in its wake.

Our daily infirmities have brought us to our knees.

Devastation from sickness and loss have our hearts bleeding.

Life as we know it has been altered.

Our personal space, if invaded, has become a possible death sentence.

Social distancing: a new valued term has been a requirement for safety.

Masks, now required for protection have become the new fashion statement.

Yet scrutinized and doubted by those who feel this is an unnecessary evil.

What was recently seen as daily freedom of movement has become shelter-in-place.

A worldwide event as our lives depends on it.

Schools have closed, students uprooted, repositioned for home learning.

Educational institutions regrouping for programs online.

Parents struggling to operate homeschooling and emulate teachers.

Small businesses struggling to stay afloat, enterprises temporarily shutting doors.

Unemployment, rising globally rivaling the great depression.

Livelihoods stricken with financial panic.

A pandemic politicized and scrutinized by world leaders, doctors, and media alike.

Mentally, we have become challenged.

Going through every emotion known to man.

Some paralyzed by the stagnation of everyday activities.

Some paralyzed by the anguish of loss.

Some darkened by loneliness and solitude.

Some withdrawing from their creative selves,

from an experience most of us have never known.

Lives have become uncomfortable.

Circumstances unbearable, straining to adapt in complicated situations.

Trying not to let anxiety consume our human psyche and resume life as usual in a reformed way.

Trying not to break from unknown variables.

Many seeking faith over fear.

Hands raised searching for answers that may never come.

Yet seeking while praising.

Looking for assurance in darkness to appear victorious in the light.

Evolving

What If

In a conversation with a friend about a poem I had written about true love, she is adamantly no longer a believer in committed relationships. She's not a fan of intimacy, but okay with relation-less companionships. She has an aversion to clingy. Her wall has been up due to an unfaithful marriage. Someone who abused her trust. She commented on her earliest dreams to be the wife and mother she could be proud of, but he destroyed her perception of what that meant.

Her feelings are relationships require too much. Love commands too much. She continues to place fault with the one who came before and the ones thereafter who destroyed her concept of what love is. She holds them accountable for her feelings of mistrust which intensifies her unwillingness to surrender herself over to love or commitment. To allow someone who may be worthy of opening her heart to behold and care for it. To become selfish in a way, to not allow another person to experience the love and intimacy she can give in return.

She, not the cuddling and affection seeking type, mentioned the idea of wanting to be the person someone could cuddle with. Yet she's still hesitant to let down the wall for fear of hurt from insincere and disenchanted men.

Since we had been discussing this subject since the end of summer, I saw an opportunity. I turned to her and posed the question, "What if?"

"What if you were to let down that wall and allow someone to have that intimacy with you? What if there was someone out there who could come into your life and be that person you're so adamant against having that relationship with?"

"What if you begin to think about the possibilities of your desire to allow someone to hold your hand in public, to look at you with affection and not be embarrassed to let others see? What if you could take his arms and wrap yourself into him, allow yourself to nestle close just to feel his warmth?"

"What if you were able to lay your head against his chest at night, listen to his heartbeat and know that it only beats for you? What if there were someone out there that could peel away the hurt you feel from the past and encourage you to feel again, trust again, love again? What if there was someone who could reach into your very soul and allow you to peer into his? What if he could be the light in your eyes when they are dim? What if you allowed this someone to show you the tenderness you so deserve and soften your once hardened heart?" I mean the possibility...

I said to her, "What if you could be with the person who is okay with you being you and him being him, and together you could share in each other's life challenges? Not above or below, but a partnership of equals. What if you could experience a type of relationship bliss where you love together, fight together, fall together, and soar together? Where nothing is perfect, but you are perfect together."

There is a chance marriage may not be your happy ending, but if you desire to be in a relationship, are you in a position to be found? He who finds, finds a good thing. Are you worth finding? What if there is a person out there who is genuine of heart to sincerely pursue you? And if there is, would you let him? Are you so caught up in past hurt that you have closed yourself off to the opportunity? Have you limited your surroundings in a way that your visual capacity is blinded by your skepticism? Are you refusing to sacrifice the fight for the closeness of what you ultimately desire? You secretly consider the idea of a meaningful relationship then renege in the very same breath.

What if there was a person who possessed the Agape kind of love which is unconditional, with the Eros kind of love that is passionate and mixed it with the Pragma kind of love that embodies friendship and compatibility? Not all people have been hurt and not all people are hurtful. It is okay to be aware and even guarded, but when will you feel safe enough to open yourself up to options?

I expressed to her that no one is perfect. Yes, love can be messy, but love is progressive. You must be open to receive it and prepared to give it. But if you love as God loves, His love is infinite.

Love is a sacrifice. Love is a test of faith. Faith is a test of patience, especially with the unknown. Love is also patient. Are you willing to open yourself up to love and be loved again when the opportunity arises, if that's your desire? When the occasion comes, will you hide and turn away or will you face and embrace it? Let the light of love shine into your heart and mind. Let the revelation of intimacy transcend your understanding of true love.

Can you see it?

So...what if?

Pains Embrace

For some time, I've dealt with infirmities I struggled to face.

My physical being was paralyzed by chronic pain.

Not something I hadn't experienced before.

I am no stranger to pain.

Pain to me is like an old acquaintance following five strides behind waiting to bump into me to make sure it's not forgotten.

I am actively functioning, pushing through every twinge while acknowledging it's there.

I am watching as others walk around with canes and use amigos to get around.

Some hunched over desiring to have perfect posture.

Struggling with their movements from normal activities, not wanting that to be me.

I am still moving forward even with the screaming ache pulsating through my frame.

The burning reminds me I am able to feel it's torture, yet I'm pushing forward not wanting it to win.

It toys with my mind trying to get me to break.

I know this is an added distraction from fulfilling my purpose.

While others continue to thrive in their craft, I have been in a perpetual funk.

My mind has been operating from a place of stillness in motion...

On autopilot.

I've been masking my feelings with a smile.

A smile distortedly staged to hide the appearances of discomfort.

Quieting the urge to express concern or complain about this unwanted pain.

Working through it, socializing through it, being doting and dutiful through it.

See, my pain disguises itself as tolerable because I say I have a high tolerance for it...until it's not.

I sometimes wrestle with it because it refuses to allow me to rest.

I could let it control me... I could lay down and take it, but I press my way through.

Medicating my pain gives me solace long enough to briefly forget it's lurking around the corner.

My pain doesn't necessarily know my name because it doesn't care where it lands.

All it knows is that my system is compromised and is susceptible to it.

It knows that if I speak its name loud enough, it will have dominion over me.

Even though I feel it, even though it humbles me and yes even fear it.

I don't want to face it.

I don't want to give it life.

I don't want to allow it to distract me from my purpose.

Although I feel like it has shunted my creative ability, I can't speak its name.

The only reason I now speak its name is to set it free.

I feel it no less, it still embraces me.

I just no longer want it to have the power to dance with me.

To be caught in its grasp.

The power to hold me hostage.

The power to stifle my creativity.

Today, I release myself from pains captivity.

Releasing Contradictions

In my head, I hear contradictions.

Listening to the two voices.

The times I question my worth.

My value as a creative.

Comparing myself to the next best thing.

I must keep repeating to myself...

I am worthy.

Worthy of success.

Worthy of greatness.

Worthy of fulfillment.

Even if I do not hear praise from those closest to me,

or they have a lackluster response to my creativity.

Being told I am extra or over my head.

Asking if the cost is worth it.

I am worth the expense.

I am the investment.

I am worth the trial and error.

While finding my way.

I am worthy of good things.

Even as my eyes are opened to the newest trends,

looking for ways to improve my brand.

I am my only competition.

I cannot look to the left or the right.

Disregarding the doubters and the naysayers.

Wondering what they think of me gets me off track.

I can only forge ahead.

If I focus on what the next person is doing,

I get swayed from carrying out my own vision.

Staying in my own lane.

Considering new ways to find inspiration.

Living up to my own expectations.

Pushing myself.

Facing myself.

Measuring my next steps.

I tell myself...

You are the next best thing.

You are uniquely qualified.

You have what it takes.

You do equate.

You are noticed.

Your voice matters.

People listen when you speak.

There is value in what you do.

Although contradictions speak to me,

I listen to those invested in me.

Those who speak life into me.

The more I speak my affirmations,

the more I separate myself from the voices inside my head.

My contradictions are only my lessons.

It is time to birth my manifestations.

Valuable Life

Life is valuable.

A treasured blessing.

We were delivered unto life as extraordinary beings,

with an inclination to develop and mature.

As human beings, we are conditioned to seek knowledge.

To gain understanding and reason justly.

To live courageously and give generously.

We can be motivated to envision beyond limitations.

To be innovators of new creations and earn insurmountable opportunities.

We are able to structure our dwellings and inhabit our surroundings.

Through this life, we're encouraged to cultivate ingenuity.

To question without repercussions and evaluate with precaution.

To walk with dignity through our struggles.

To love unapologetically and protect emphatically.

In this life, we aspire to empower the powerless and boldly engage.

To penetrate the minds of those with whom we connect.

To recognize the power of that which we generate.

We endeavor to spawn the procreation of the next generation.

To establish stability in an unstable reality.

To earnestly learn essential life lessons.

Life is valuable.

A gift from our creator not to be wasted.

Protected from the kleptomaniac

that wishes to snuff out the light which is our life.

Pregnant Dreams

One night, I dreamt I was pregnant. I felt the weight of carrying what I thought was a child. Feeling the warmth and movement of life. I also felt the pressure to deliver. The feeling was so real until I woke from the dream. Feeling something, that during my waking moments lay dormant from any procreated life at all.

I was upset at this thought because as much as I had longed for a child, it brought back memories of a previous miscarriage. A life aborted before an attached excitement could begin. In turn, I felt I couldn't physically carry one to term because of my age, lupus diagnosis as well as other medical challenges. I'd decided it would be an unfulfilled dream.

I had once longed to see what a mini-me would be like. How it would grow, and I'd nurture and teach— have shared moments with. Maybe I felt the emotions of emptiness because it would never be.

As I pondered it, I realized being pregnant had nothing to do with birthing a physical child but had everything to do with birthing purpose. I was pregnant with purpose, but what was my purpose?

I believed myself to be in the gestational period; to carry something. To produce something. I was challenging myself to step out and do things I would have never done before. Holding life in my hands before experiencing it. Before waking to life around me and not restricting my own growth. I was discovering things about myself that were in hibernation. New nuances of a person I'm still getting to know.

I believe my dream was showing me the purpose of anticipation. Anticipation of birthing my first works and the second and what came after. Anticipation of new directions and more to come. With anticipation comes revelation of new ideas. Creativity taking different strides than ideas before it. Seeing the flourishing strokes of artistry to that of the unknown.

Like life continues to evolve, my purpose was continuing to evolve. The birth of a new voice opens doors for planted seeds. To watch opportunities, open and develop within those opportunities. The birth of a new identity. To see the life of another take root in my own personality for the good and enjoyment of those around me. The exploration of new ideas and seeing the seduction of the vision being birthed. The planting of wisdom within my own circle to enlighten and encourage those around me.

My dream of being pregnant was a precursor for things to come. Preparing me for self-rebirth. My mind had been fertilizing planted seeds. It was preparing me for the forthcoming fruit. My mind was waiting for my body to gain the traction it needed to produce the offspring of my dreams.

Reflections

Each night I closed my eyes to go to sleep,

I pray morning will come.

That when my eyes open, I will see things anew.

That I'll have another opportunity to right any wrongs.

To speak the truth.

To love you through.

To love in quiet times.

To value in desperate times.

To honor not only you, but most importantly, me too.

To appreciate the small things.

Celebrate the large ones.

That my smile brings light.

That He shines through.

Those things I touch, create joy in life.

I pray that yesterday's reflections generate daily affirmations.

That divine inspiration prepares me for tomorrow's successes.

I pray that I live life, but the experience of life doesn't live me.

I pray that confidence is not my shadow but my reflection.

I pray each moment; I live to cherish.

Every breath taken; I appreciate the gift of life.

And prayerfully, regret will not part from my lips.

Available Books

Spiritual Thoughts Intimate Expressions:
An Inspirational and Reflective Book of Poetry

Images of Me:
Poetry and Reflective Compositions

Coming Soon

Rose Petals and Embers:
Poetic Short Stories for Lovers

About the Author

For more than 20 years, she's been inspiring, motivating and empowering others by the written word and her creative gifts. A creative genius in her own right, Nikí Ferguson, author and poet, uses her hands to create literary work for people worldwide. Though soft-spoken and meek, Niki gives a voice to those who may feel like they have lost theirs along the way. When performing at an open mic night, her artistic voice speaks loud and clear when she uses her platform to allow others to experience it. Using her voice as a catalyst of change, Niki seeks to prick the heart of every reader, ushering them into deep thought, emotional healing, and a spiritual abyss.

Through her poetic prose, she sparks conversations of interest and controversy, making the words on the pages come to life in the room. Even long after she's done speaking, listeners hold a sincere, intimate piece of her heart that cannot be taken away. In addition to her debut project, *Spiritual Thoughts, Intimate Expressions*, her sophomore project, *Images of Me*, and now her current release, *Illuminated Soul*, it is not uncommon for supporters to purchase her signature framed poetry pieces as gifts or home accents—serving as a thermostat of change for the environment in which it sits. Her clients rave about her warm, welcoming spirit and describe her as "one in a million."

For more information or interviews, email simplynikicreations@gmail.com. Connect with her on Facebook at SimplyNikiPoetry, SimplyNikiCreations and on Instagram at @simplynikicreations. You can also find out more about her services and products at NikiRFerguson.com.

Look for her upcoming project, *Rose Petals and Embers* under her alias Karama.